Frank Schaffer Publications®

Printed in the United States of America. All rights reserved. Limited Reproduction Permission: Permission to duplicate these materials is limited to the person for whom they are purchased. Reproduction for an entire school or school district is unlawful and strictly prohibited. Frank Schaffer Publications is an imprint of School Specialty Publishing. Copyright © 2006 School Specialty Publishing.

Send all inquiries to:
Frank Schaffer Publications
3195 Wilson Drive NW
Grand Rapids, Michigan 49534

Spanish—Grade 1

ISBN 0-7696-8241-3

1 2 3 4 5 6 7 8 9 10 WAL 10 09 08 07 06

Table of Contents

Numbers 4	The Face 41
Numbers 5	The Face 42
Numbers 1–5 6	What's on Your Face? 43
Matching Review 7	Family 44
Matching Numbers 8	Family 45
Number the Stars 9	Family Words 46
1–10 Matching 10	My Family 47
Count the Cookies 11	Community 48
My Favorite Number 12	Community 49
Circles 1–10 13	Places to Go 50
Coloring 0–10 14	Our Town 51
Spanish Alphabet 15	Classroom Objects 52
Listening Practice 16	Classroom Objects 53
Parts of Speech 17	Classroom Things 54
Parts of Speech 18	Matching Objects 55
Introductions and Greetings 19	Songs and Chants 56
Introductions and Greetings 20	Songs and Chants 57
Introductions and Greetings 21	Songs and Chants 58
Pictures of Greetings 22	Songs and Chants 59
Days 23	Songs and Chants 60
Months 24	Numbers 61
Seven Days 25	Numbers 62
Colors 26	Numbers 63
Colors 27	Numbers 64
Colors Introduction 28	The Face 65
Food 29	The Face 66
Food 30	Colors 67
Food and Drink 31	Colors 68
My Meal 32	Colors and Food 69
Animals 33	Colors and Food 70
Animals 34	Food 71
Animal Crossword 35	Food 72
Clothing 36	Food 73
Clothing 37	Food 74
Clothing 38	Family 75
Clothing Match-Ups 39	Family 76
How Are You? 40	Answer Key 77–80

Name _____

Numbers

uno

dos

tres

cuatro

cinco

Name _____

Numbers

seis

siete

8
ocho

nueve

diez

Name _____

Numbers 1–5

Say each word out loud.

uno		1

dos			2

tres				3

cuatro					4

cinco						5

Published by Frank Schaffer Publications. Copyright protected.   Spanish: Grade 1

Name _____

Numbers Review

Write the number next to the Spanish word. Circle the correct number of animals for each number shown. Then, color the pictures.

uno

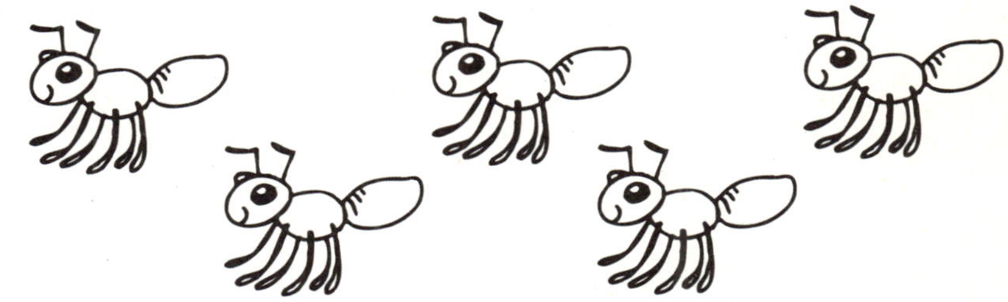

cinco

dos

cuatro

tres

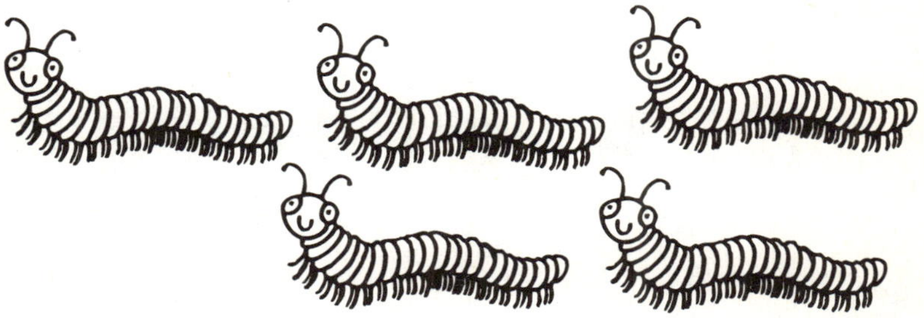

7

Published by Frank Schaffer Publications. Copyright protected.

Spanish: Grade 1

Matching Numbers

Draw a line from the word to the correct picture. Then, color the pictures.

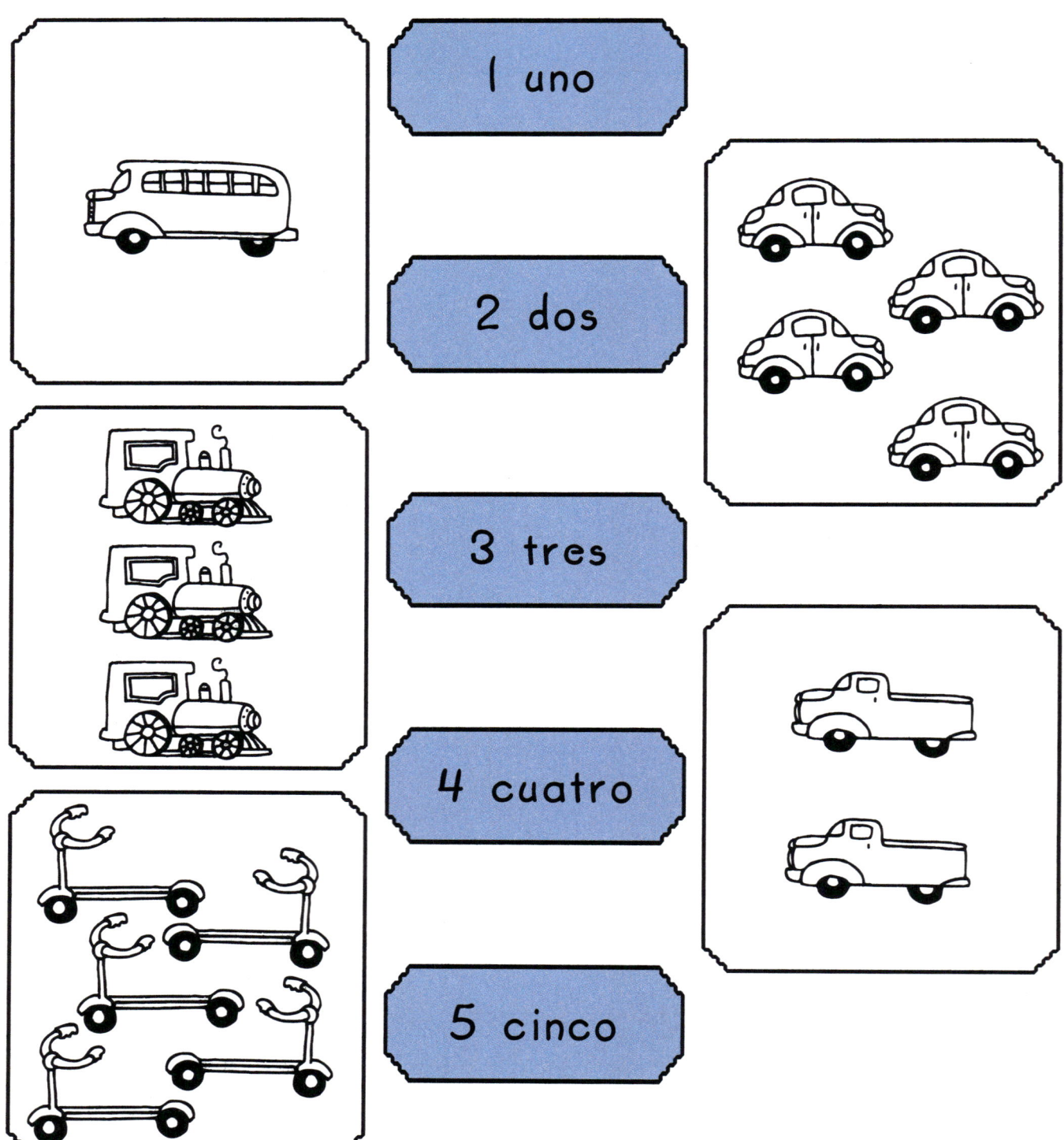

Name _____

Number the Stars

Draw the correct number of stars next to each number.

uno

dos

tres

cuatro

cinco

Name _____

1–10 Matching

Draw a line to match each object to the number that is written in Spanish.

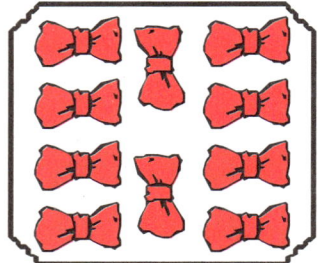

uno	1
dos	2
tres	3
cuatro	4
cinco	5
seis	6
siete	7
ocho	8
nueve	9
diez	10

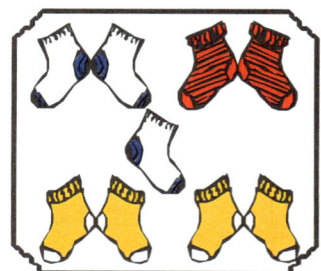

Count the Cookies

Name _____

In each box at the left, write the number that matches the Spanish word. Cross out the correct number of cookies to show the number written in Spanish. The first one is done for you.

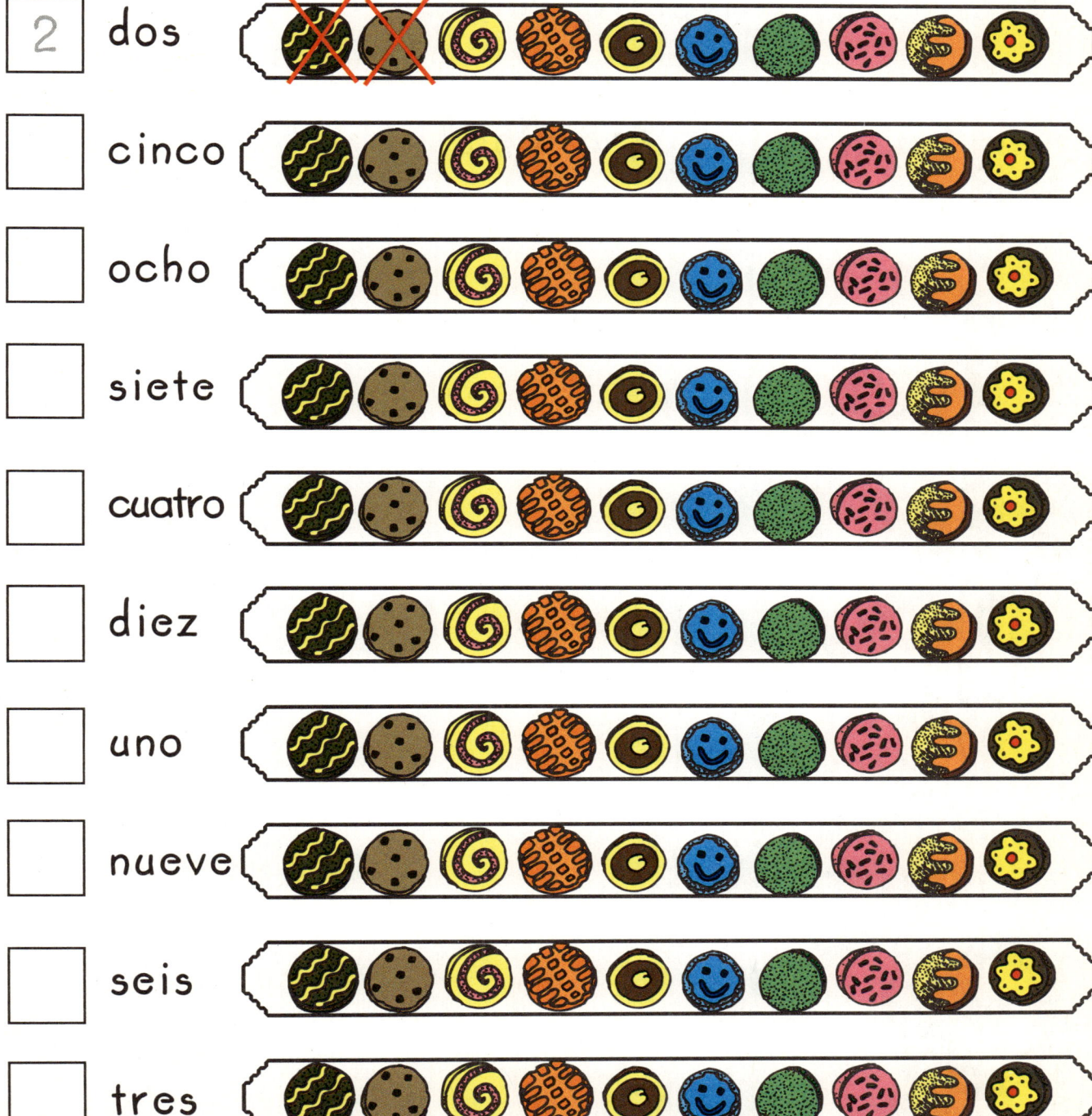

Published by Frank Schaffer Publications. Copyright protected.

Spanish: Grade 1

Name _____

My Favorite Number

Write your favorite number from 1 to 10 in the boxes. Draw a picture to show that number.

My favorite number is ☐.

In Spanish, it is called ☐.

Published by Frank Schaffer Publications. Copyright protected. Spanish: Grade 1

Name_____

Circles 1–10

Draw the correct number of circles in each box.

uno		seis	
dos		siete	
tres		ocho	
cuatro		nueve	
cinco		diez	

Name _____

Coloring 0–10

Color or circle the number of butterflies that shows the number written in Spanish.

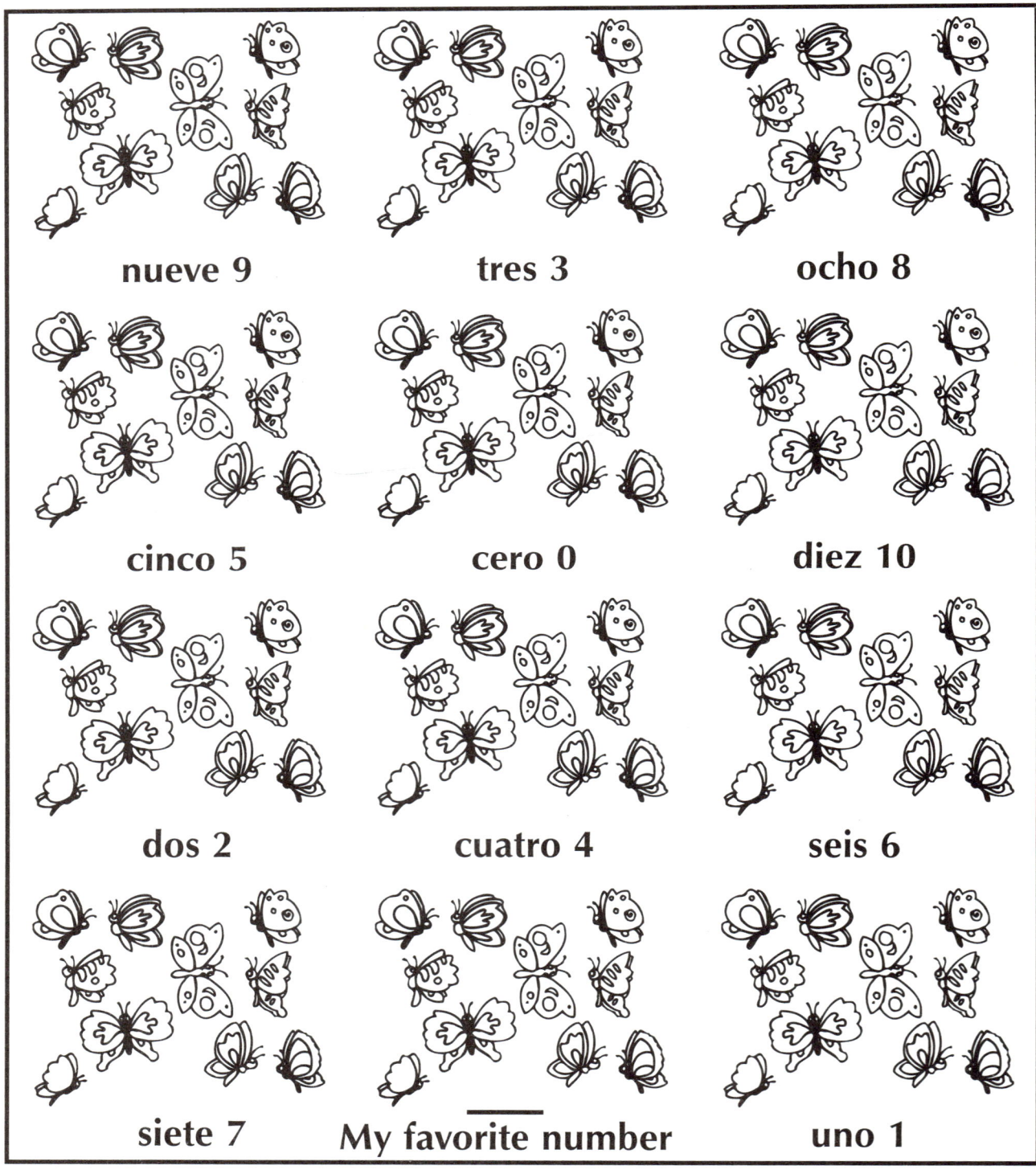

14

Published by Frank Schaffer Publications. Copyright protected.

Spanish: Grade 1

Spanish Alphabet

EL ABECEDARIO (EL ALFABETO) EN ESPAÑOL

Aa	a	Jj	jota	Rr	ere
Bb	be	Kk	ka	Ss	ese
Cc	ce	Ll	ele	Tt	te
Dd	de	Mm	eme	Uu	u
Ee	e	Nn	ene	Vv	ve
Ff	efe	Ññ	eñe	Ww	doble ve
Gg	ge	Oo	o	Xx	equis
Hh	hache	Pp	pe	Yy	i griega
Ii	i	Qq	cu	Zz	zeta

Rhyming Vowel Practice

Say these sentences out loud:

A, E, I, O U, ¡Más sabe el burro que tú!

A, E, I, O, U, ¿Cuántos años tienes tú?

Name _____

Listening Practice

Say the Spanish word for each number out loud.
Write the first letter of the words you hear.

1 _____   4 _____   7 _____

2 _____   5 _____   8 _____

3 _____   6 _____   9 _____

Color the letters of the Spanish alphabet. Say them in Spanish as you color them.

A B C D E F G
H I J K L M N
Ñ O P Q R S T
U V W X Y Z

Name _____

Parts of Speech

tú

usted

pretty

bonita

ugly

feo

Published by Frank Schaffer Publications. Copyright protected.

Name _____

Parts of Speech

happy

alegre

to read

leer

sad

triste

to play

jugar

to eat

comer

Introductions and Greetings

¡Hola!

¿Cómo te llamas?

Me llamo...

Introductions and Greetings

 ¿Cómo estás?

bien

así, así

¡Adiós!

mal

Name _____

Days

lunes   miércoles   viernes   domingo

martes   jueves   sábado

Monday	Tuesday	Wednesday	Thursday	Friday	Saturday	Sunday
		1	2	3	4	5
6	7	8	9	10	11	12
13	14	15	16	17	18	19
20	21	22	23	24	25	26
27	28	29	30			

Months

Seven Days

Copy the Spanish words for the days of the week. In Spanish-speaking countries, *lunes* is the first day of the week.

Monday	**lunes**	_____
Tuesday	**martes**	_____
Wednesday	**miércoles**	_____
Thursday	**jueves**	_____
Friday	**viernes**	_____
Saturday	**sábado**	_____
Sunday	**domingo**	_____

Draw a line to match the Spanish and English days of the week.

Name _____

Colors

Name _____

Colors

café

anaranjado

morado

rojo

rosado

Name _____

Colors Introduction

Say the words out loud. Color the word with the correct color.

Name _____

Food

leche

pollo

ensalada

Name _____

Food

queso

papa

pan

jugo

Name _____

Food and Drink

Say the Spanish words for some delicious foods and drinks out loud.

| queso |  | cheese |

| leche |  | milk |

| papa |  | potato |

| jugo |  | juice |

| pan | 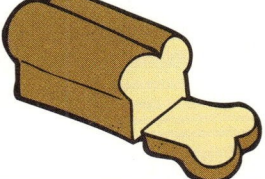 | bread |

| pollo |  | chicken |

| ensalada |  | salad |

Name _____

My Meal

Draw or cut out pictures of food and glue them on the plate to make a meal. Which food is your favorite?

Mi comida

Name _____

Animals

perro

pájaro

rana

pez

vaca

Name _____

Animals

abeja

pato

gato

oso

caballo

Name _____

Animal Crossword

Use the picture clues to complete the puzzle. Choose from the Spanish words at the bottom of the page. One is done for you.

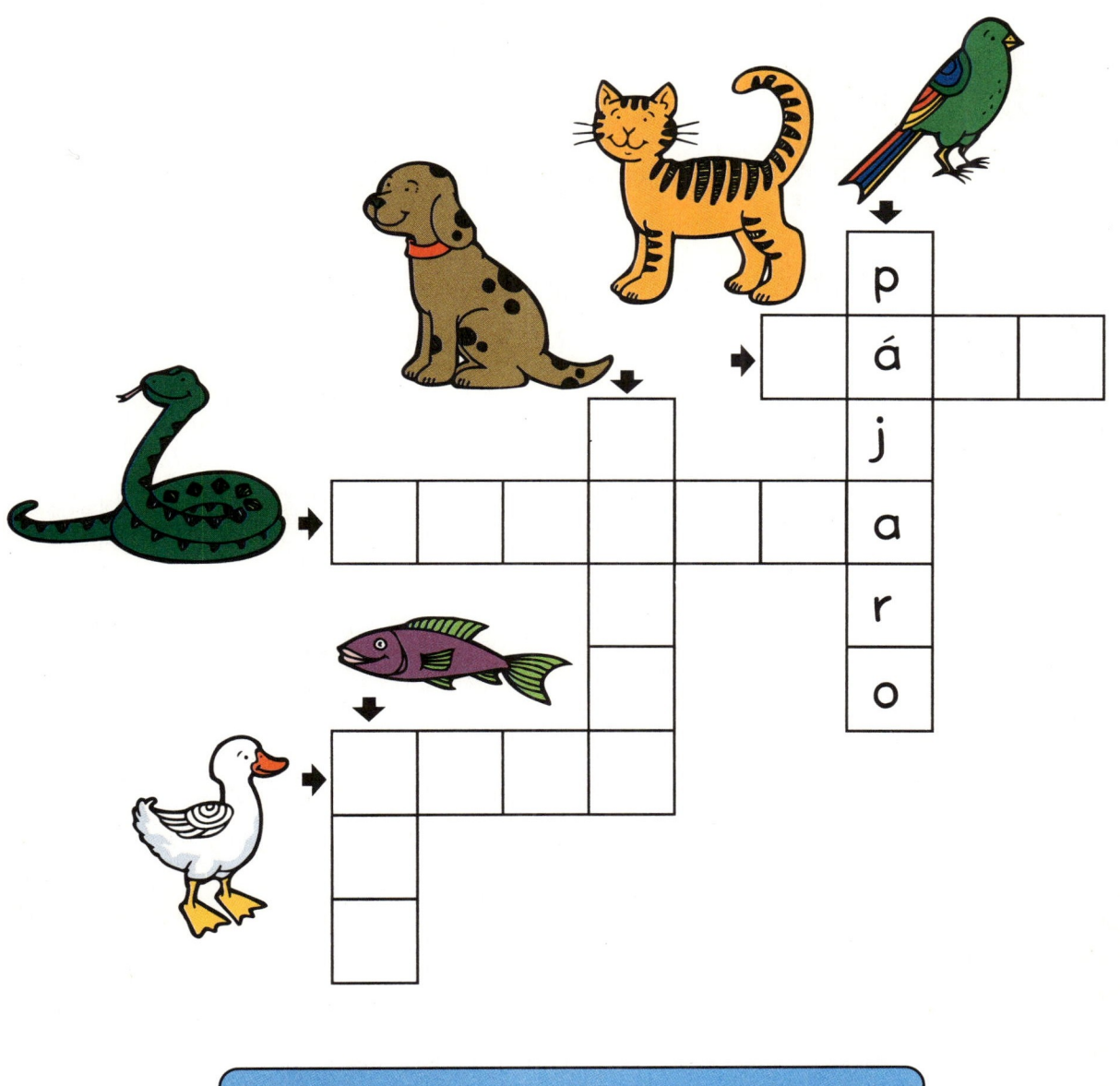

| gato | perro | pájaro |
| pez | pato | culebra |

Clothing

Name _____

Clothing

calcetines

zapatos

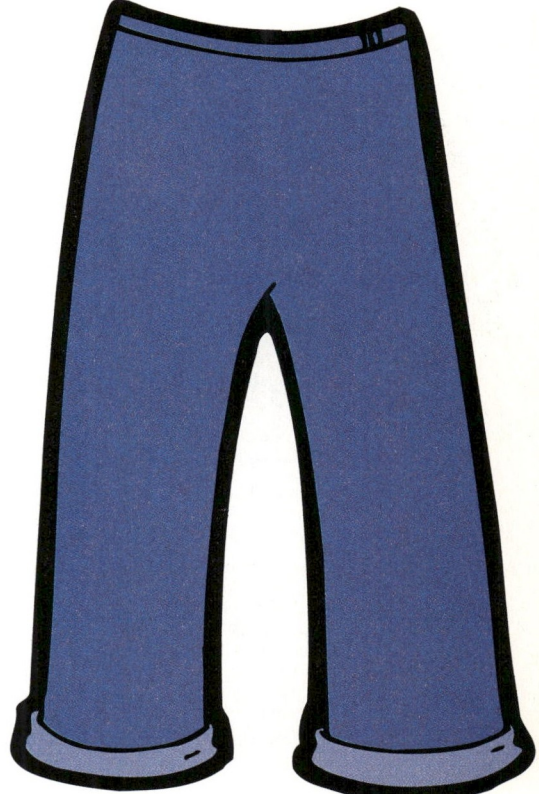

pantalones

Name _____

Clothing

Say each word out loud.

| camisa |  | shirt |

| pantalones |  | pants |

| vestido |  | dress |

| calcetines |  | socks |

| zapatos |  | shoes |

| gorro |  | cap |

Name _____

Clothing Match-Ups

Draw a line from the word to the correct picture. Color the picture.

camisa

pantalones

zapatos

gorro

vestido

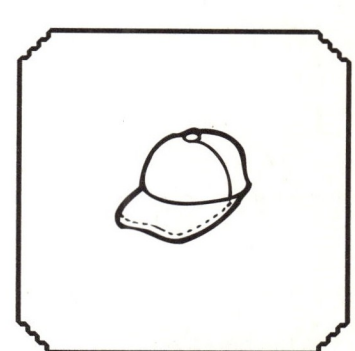

calcetines

How Are You?

Name _____

Draw or cut out pictures of clothes to make a boy or girl. Write the names of the clothes next to them in Spanish.

Name _____

The Face

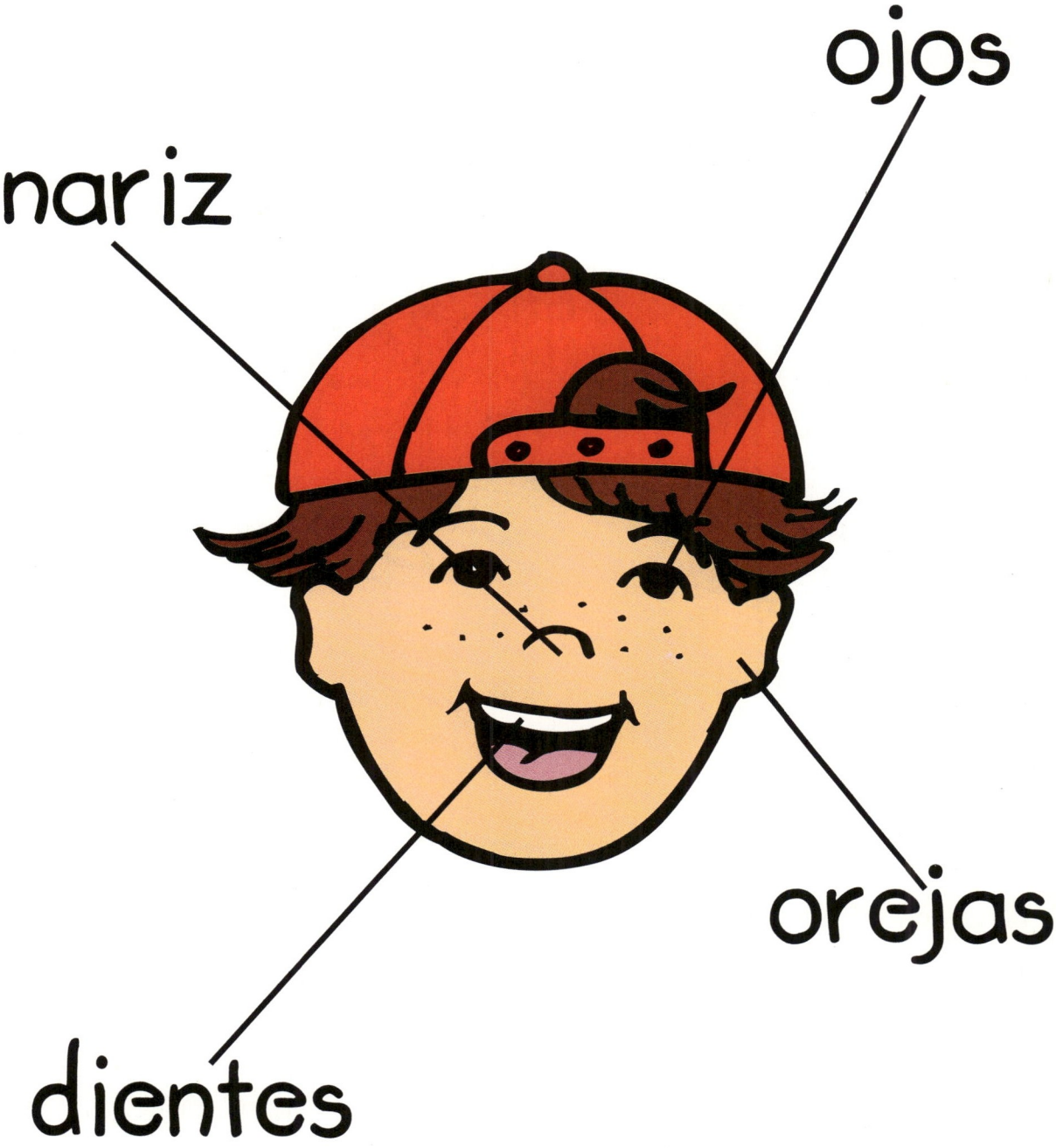

Name _____

The Face

What's on Your Face?

Say each word out loud. Copy each word.

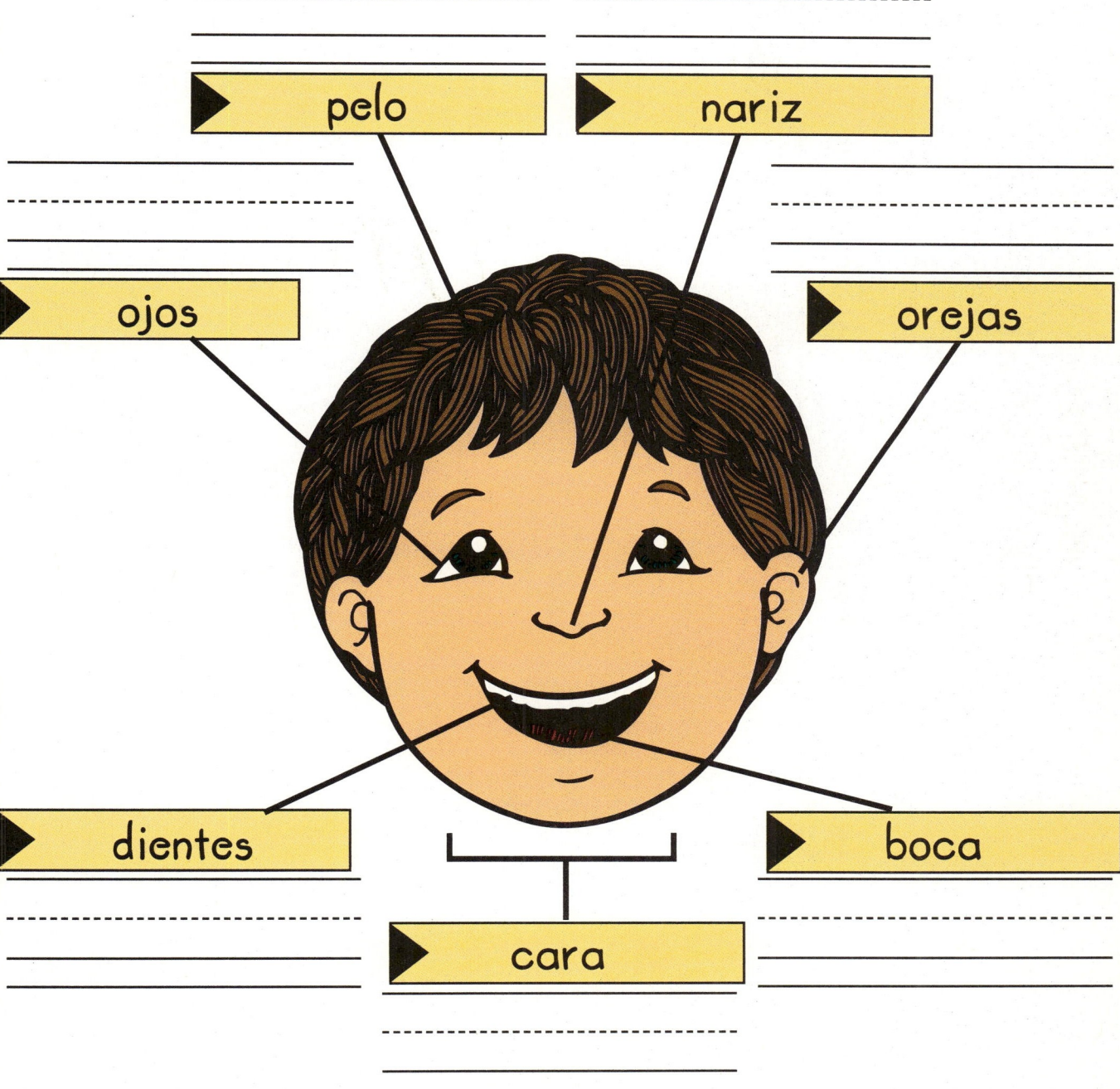

Which part of your face do you like the best? _____

Name _____

Family

padre

madre

hermano

Family

hermana

abuela

abuelo

Name _____

Family Words

Say each family word out loud.

| madre |  | mother |

| padre |  | father |

| hermana |  | sister |

| hermano |  | brother |

| abuela |  | grandmother |

| abuelo |  | grandfather |

Published by Frank Schaffer Publications. Copyright protected.

Spanish: Grade 1

Name _____

My Family

Draw a picture of your family. Color your picture.

Mi familia

Write the correct Spanish word next to each person in your picture above.

| padre | hermano | abuelo |
| madre | hermana | abuela |

Spanish: Grade 1

Community

biblioteca

escuela

parque

Name _____

Community

tienda

casa

museo

Name _____

Places to Go

Say the Spanish words out loud.

escuela		school
museo		museum
casa		house
tienda		store
biblioteca		library
parque		park

Name _____

Our Town

Draw a picture of a town showing the community places named at the bottom of the page. Label the places in Spanish.

escuela   museo   casa
biblioteca   tienda   parque

Classroom Objects

Name _____

Classroom Objects

borrador

mesa

silla

Classroom Things

Say each word out loud.

silla		chair
libro		book
mesa		table
lápiz		pencil
tijeras		scissors
borrador	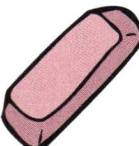	eraser

Name _____

Matching Objects

Draw a line from the word to the correct picture. Color the picture.

silla

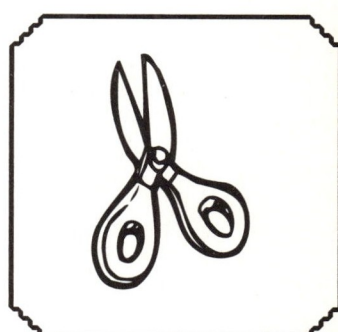

libro

mesa

lápiz

tijeras

borrador

Songs and Chants

¡Hola! Means Hello
(to the tune of "London Bridge")

¡Hola! means hello-o-o, hello-o-o, hello-o-o.
¡Hola! means hello-o-o. ¡Hola, amigos!

¡Adiós! Means Good-bye
(to the tune of "London Bridge")

¡Adiós! means goo-ood-bye, goo-ood-bye, goo-ood-bye.
¡Adiós! means goo-ood-bye. ¡Adiós, amigos!

Cinco amigos
(to the tune of "Ten Little Fingers")

Uno, dos, tres, cuatro, cinco,
Uno, dos, tres, cuatro, cinco,
Uno, dos, tres, cuatro, cinco,
Cinco amigos son.

Introductions and Greetings

Say the Spanish introductions and greetings out loud.

| ¡Hola! |  | Hello |

| ¿Cómo te llamas? |  | What is your name? |

| Me llamo… |  | My name is… |

| ¿Cómo estás?.. |  | How are you? |

|  |  |  |
| bien | mal | así, así |

| ¡Adiós! |   | Good-bye |

Pictures of Greetings

Say the greeting out loud. Circle the picture that tells the meaning of each word.

| ¡Hola! |  |  |

| ¿Cómo te llamas? |  |  |

| Me llamo... |   |  |

| ¿Cómo estás? |  |  |

| bien |  |  |

| mal |  |  |

| así, así |  |  |

| ¡Adiós! |  |  |

Songs and Chants

Diez amigos
(to the tune of "Ten Little Fingers")

Uno, dos, tres amigos,
cuatro, cinco, seis amigos,
siete, ocho, nueve amigos,
diez amigos son.

Diez, nueve, ocho amigos,
siete, seis, cinco amigos,
cuatro, tres, dos amigos,
un amigo es.

Colors Song
(to the tune of "Twinke, Twinkle Little Star")

Red is rojo,   green is verde,
purple, morado,   brown, café;
yellow, amarillo,   blue, azul,
pink is rosado,   orange, anaranjado;
white is blanco,   black is negro,
colors, colores,   colors, colores.

Name _____

Songs and Chants

Classroom Objects Song

(to the tune of "The Farmer in the Dell")

A silla is a chair;
A libro is a book;
A mesa is a table in our classroom.

A lápiz is a pencil;
Tijeras are scissors;
A borrador is an eraser in our classroom.

Clothing Song

(to the tune of "Skip to My Lou")

Camisa — shirt, pantalones — pants,
vestido — dress, calcetines — socks,
zapatos — shoes, gorro — cap
These are the clothes that we wear.

Songs and Chants

Family Song
(to the tune of "Are You Sleeping?")

Padre — father,
madre — mother,
chico — boy,
chica — girl,
abuelo is grandpa,
abuela is grandma.
Our family, our family.

Hermano — brother,
hermana — sister,
chico — boy,
chica — girl,
padre y madre,
abuelo y abuela.
Our family, our family.

Clothing Song
(to the tune of "Skip to My Lou")

Camisa — shirt, *pantalones* — pants,
vestido — dress, *calcetines* — socks,
zapatos — shoes, *gorro* — cap.
These are the clothes that we wear.

Chaqueta — jacket, *botas* — boots,
abrigo — dress, *falda* — skirt,
guantes are gloves. What did we forget?
Pantalones cortos are shorts.

Animals Song
(to the tune of "This Old Man")

Gato — cat,
perro — dog,
pájaro is a flying bird,
pez is a fish, and
pato is a duck,
culebra is a slinky snake.

Songs and Chants

Community Song
(to the tune of "Here We Go 'Round the Mulberry Bush")

Escuela is school,
museo — museum,
casa is house,
tienda is store,
biblioteca is library,
parque is the park for me!

Alphabet Song
(to the tune of "B-I-N-G-O")

A	B	C	D	E	F	G
(There	was	a	farmer	had	a	dog)

H		I	J		K	
(and Bin-		go	was his		name-o.)	

L	M	N	Ñ	O
(B	I	N	G	O)

P	Q	R	S	T
(B	I	N	G	O)

U	V	W		
(B	I	N G O)		

X	Y		Z	
(and	Bingo was his		name-o.)	

Name _____

Numbers

0 cero	1 uno 
2 dos 	3 tres
4 cuatro 	5 cinco 

Spanish: Grade 1

This page is intentionally left blank.

Name _____

Numbers and the Face

6 seis

7 siete

8 ocho

9 nueve

10 diez

cara

This page is intentionally left blank.

The Face

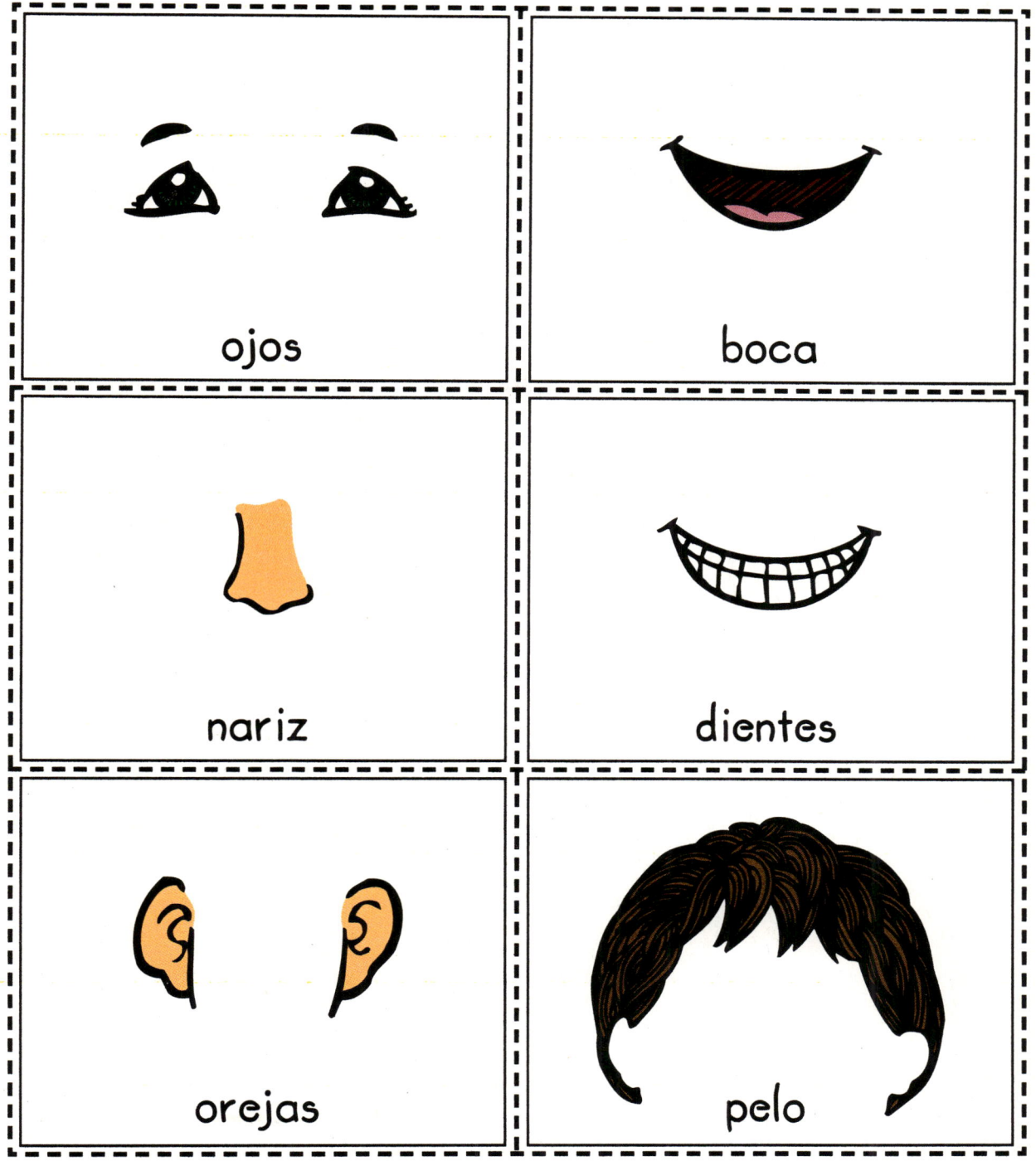

This page is intentionally left blank.

Name _____

Colors

This page is intentionally left blank.

Name _____

Colors and Food

This page is intentionally left blank.

Food

This page is intentionally left blank.

Food

This page is intentionally left blank.

Name _____

Family

This page is intentionally left blank.

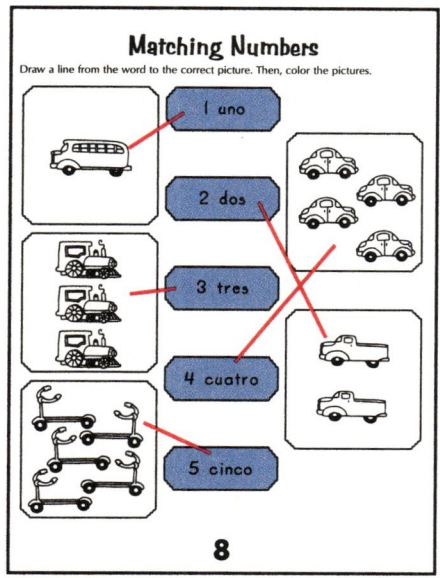

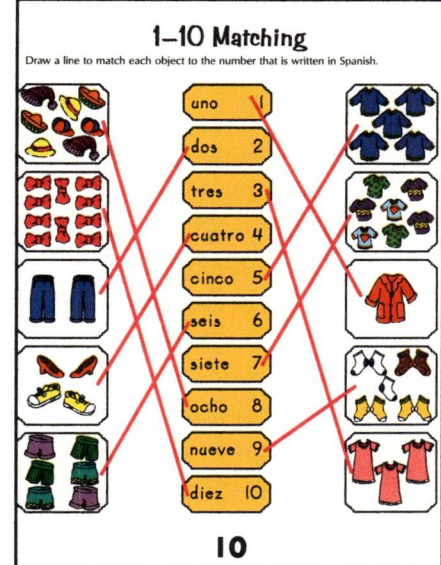
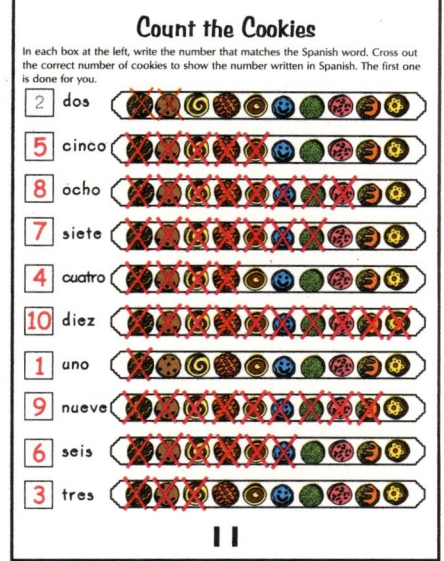

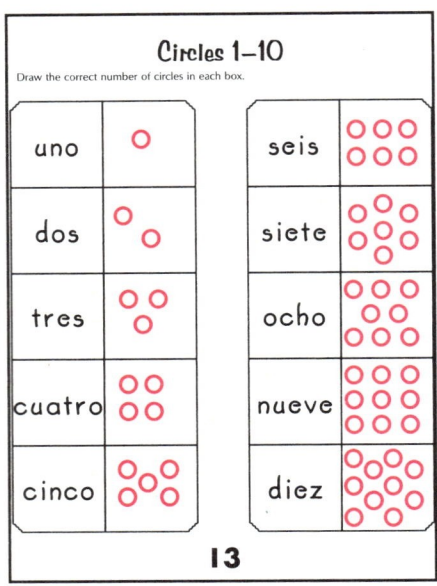
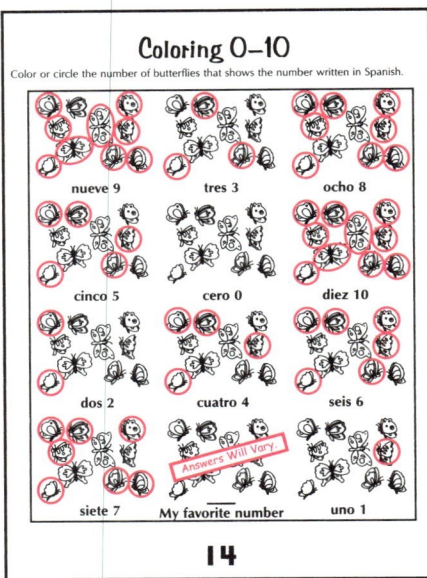
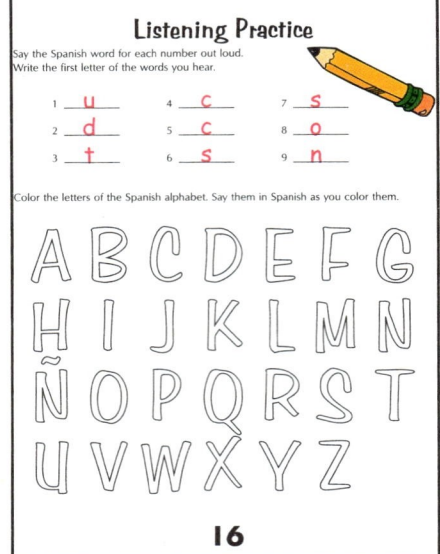

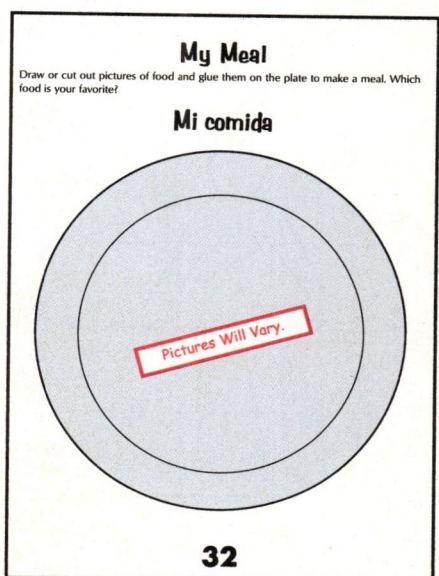
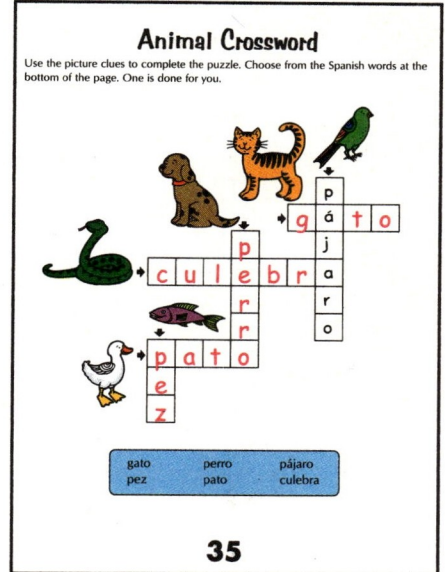
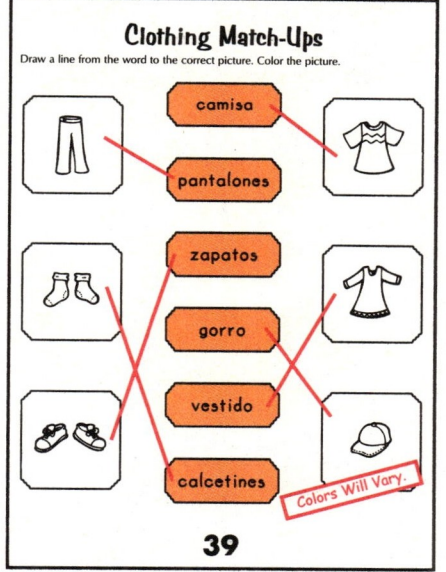

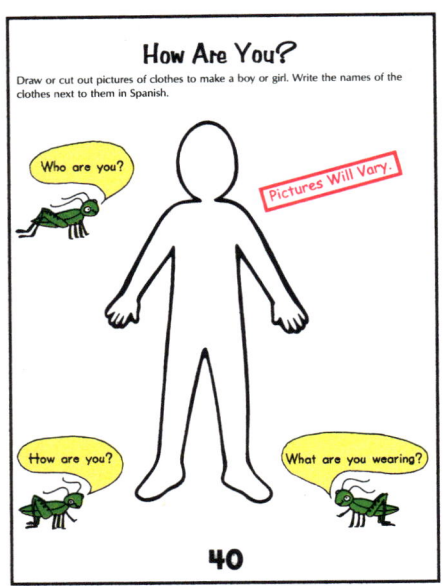
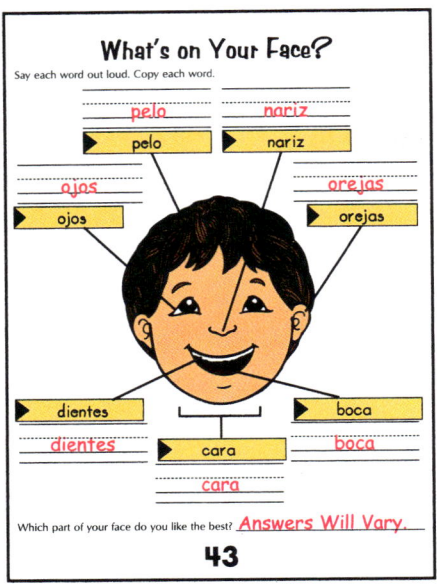

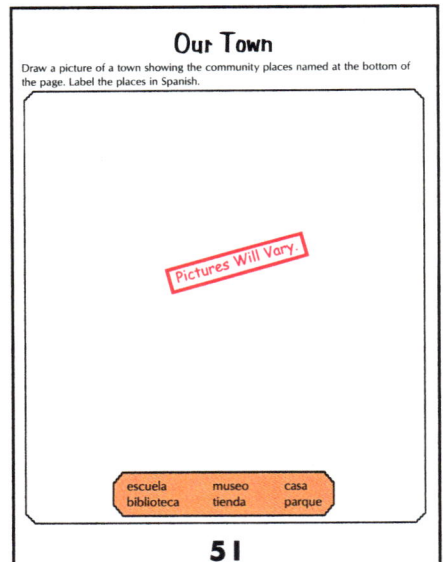
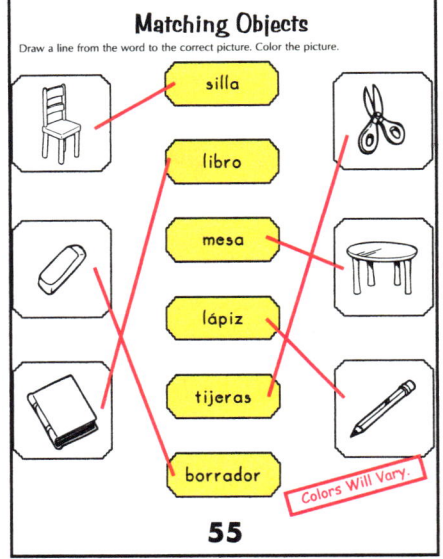